VICTORIAN PUMPING STATIONS

Trevor Yorke

SHIRE PUBLICATIONS
Bloomsbury Publishing Plc

Kemp House, Chawley Park, Oxford OX2 9PH, UK
29 Earlsfort Terrace, Dublin 2, Ireland
1385 Broadway, 5th Flr, New York, NY 10018, USA
Email: shire@bloomsbury.com
www.shirebooks.co.uk

SHIRE is a trademark of Osprey Publishing Ltd

First published in Great Britain in 2018
Transferred to digital print in 2023

Shire Library no. 846
Print ISBN: 978 1 78442 268 4
ePub: 978 1 78442 267 7
ePDF: 978 1 78442 266 0
XML: 978 1 78442 265 3

Typeset by PDQ Digital Media Solutions, Bungay, UK
Printed and bound in India by Replika Press Private Ltd.

FSC
MIX
Paper from
responsible sources
FSC® C016779
www.fsc.org

24 25 26 27   10 9 8 7 6 5 4 3

The Woodland Trust
Shire Publications supports the Woodland Trust, the
UK's leading woodland conservation charity.

www.shirebooks.co.uk
To find out more about our authors and books visit our
website. Here you will find extracts, author interviews,
details of forthcoming events and the option to sign-up
for our newsletter.

Cover image
Front cover: The restored beam steam engine and cast
ironwork at the Crossness Pumping Station.

Title page image
This exotic Victorian pumping station at Abbey Mills
in East London has colourful Gothic Revival pointed
arches and detailing and a hint of Moorish architecture
in its unusual form. Its plan is in the shape of a Greek
cross and the building originally housed a pair of steam
beam engines in each arm.

Contents page image
The engine and boiler house at Crossness Pumping
Station, inspired by Norman architecture, are open to
the public on certain weekends through the year. One
of the capitals on the columns between the windows
features the face of civil engineer Joseph Bazalgette.

Acknowledgements
Pictures are acknowledged as follows: Alamy, front
cover and pages 17 (top left) and 30 (top); Wikimedia
Commons/The Voice of the Hassocks, page 40
(top right).

All other images are copyright of the author.

CONTENTS

THE VICTORIAN PUMPING STATION

S TEAM-POWERED PUMPING STATIONS with their rich decorative architecture and mighty beam engines are amongst the most distinctive and important buildings of the nineteenth century. They were built to drain agricultural land and improve production, top up the water in canals to keep commercial traffic moving, and supply the hydraulic systems that powered industrial machinery. The most impressive, however, were erected as part of revolutionary, large-scale water supply and sewage disposal systems, which significantly improved the health of the nation. Before looking in detail at these intriguing buildings we will briefly explain why these ornate municipal pumping stations came into being in the first place.

The population of industrial towns and cities was booming in the early nineteenth century. In the first three decades Liverpool grew from 82,000 to 202,000, Leeds from 53,000 to 123,000 and London from around 1,000,000 to 1,730,000 inhabitants. Most of them were squeezed into accommodation without clean running water and effective methods of waste disposal. The situation was made even worse because many who moved from the country brought their livestock with them. Inevitably, disease became rampant in working-class areas as the continued demand for housing overwhelmed the existing utilities and created the notorious Victorian slums.

The initial lack of action in dealing with these problems was partly due to the ethos of 'self help', which resulted in the

Great pride was taken in the huge steam-powered beam engines that operated the pumps. This beautifully maintained example at Papplewick Pumping Station formerly supplied water to Nottingham.

authorities resisting calls for action. They were content to let local corporate initiative take the lead and were reluctant to pass legislation unless the situation became so chaotic that it would restrict enterprise. Improvements to water supply and sewage were also hindered by people's misunderstanding of the ways in which disease could be spread; until the second half of the nineteenth century most people believed in the 'miasma' theory – the idea that deadly outbreaks were caused by poisonous particles of decaying matter in foul-smelling air. The word 'malaria' is derived from the Italian words *mala* and *aria* (bad air), since this was believed to be the source of the disease. The fact that unpleasant odours seemed to hang over the slum areas where epidemics were centred only added weight to the theory.

One of the first to disprove this idea was Dr John Snow. Whilst working in London during the cholera epidemic of 1849 he studied an outbreak in the south of the city and realised that the water supply was being contaminated by cesspits in the rear of the properties during heavy rainfall, and that the disease broke out shortly afterwards. He made a similar study in 1854 in Soho, plotting the occurrences of the disease and tracing it back to a water pump in Broad Street (now Broadwick Street). Once he had the handle removed the number of cholera cases quickly subsided. Although his theory that the disease was water-bound would not be proven until the 1880s, his voice was one amongst a growing number calling for action to improve the quality of drinking water and create an effective sewage system.

Mounting pressure upon the government came not just from these vocal campaigners: there were by now hard facts and detailed reports that would force their hand. The census, first carried out in 1801 and by 1841 recording full details about individuals and their occupations, clearly illustrated the population shift and where it was most dense; photographs recorded the slum conditions in which many were living. An increasing number of Royal Commissions were set up, which could be shocking in their detail and led to undeniable

One of the earliest uses of steam-powered pumps was to top up the summit level of canals. The original 200-year-old Boulton and Watt steam engine at Crofton Pumping Station, Wiltshire, still supplies water to the Kennet and Avon Canal.

conclusions. A new official, the inspector, became key in highlighting the plight of the working classes at a local level. One such man, Robert Rawlinson, was sent to look into the sanitary conditions in Sunderland in 1850 and published a report in the following year which opened the eyes of those in authority to the shocking state of poor housing in the area. He described a cottage whose walls were constantly wet and which stood next to large mounds of manure and recalled, 'When I first visited this cottage I found it occupied by a very clean old woman and her husband; their bedroom was very offensive; they are both since dead of cholera.'

As a result of this growing weight of information, local and national government passed legislation that would ultimately result in the authorities taking responsibility for public utilities. The 1835 Municipal Corporation Act reformed over 170 boroughs across the country (excluding London, which had its own reforms) and established town councils elected by ratepayers. The 1848 Public Health Act enabled those boroughs that had formed a corporation to take responsibility for water supply and sewage removal. Loans were made available for new infrastructure, which could be paid back through the local rates. This produced a patchy reform, as the actions were not compulsory; however, legislation driven through by the Chief Medical Officer, John Simon, during the 1860s and '70s was more effective. The 1866 Sanitary Act permitted the government to overrule local authorities on matters of health, and the 1872 and 1875 Public Health Acts divided the country into districts and established sanitary inspectors and medical officers

Agricultural production was increased in many areas by the introduction of steam engines to aid land drainage. The Hundred Foot Pumping Station at Pymoor, Cambridgeshire, was built in 1830 to replace wind pumps, which had been overwhelmed by flooding a few years earlier.

in each, with powers in matters of water and sewage.

The result was the construction of new water supply and sewage removal systems. Initially, private companies established most of these, but later in the century public authorities were more active and used the legislation to buy the former out and improve the service. Many of these projects involved major civil engineering works with huge dams, miles of pipework and sewers, and large-scale filter beds and storage reservoirs. However, the key to making these new systems work were the pumping stations, which raised water and sewage at various points along a route. Without their reliable steam-powered beam engines and efficient pumps none of these improvements in health would have been possible.

The former Park Works, The Ropewalk, Nottingham was designed by the pioneering engineer Thomas Hawksley.

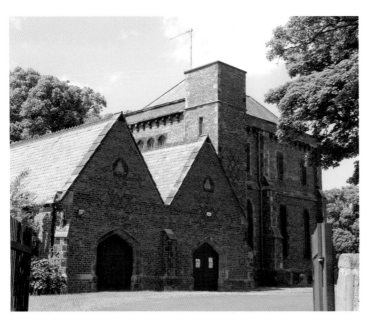

It was mainly in the industrial towns and cities of the Midlands and North of England where legislation was first used to improve water supply. Fulwell Pumping Station, Sunderland, was built to the designs of Thomas Hawksley in 1852.

THE BUILDINGS

THE IMPRESSIVE STRUCTURE of Victorian pumping stations reflected the shape and space required for the beam engines and boilers they housed. Even where the designer of the buildings chose to imitate an exotic temple or medieval castle, its form was still guided by the mechanical parts inside. The engine house had to be tall where it accommodated a beam engine, the boiler room wide enough to cover the line of boilers that provided the steam, and the coal store large enough to contain the vast quantities of fuel consumed by the pumping stations. The position of each part in relation to the others reflects the order of the process of producing steam and powering the pumps.

The tall engine house enclosed the beam engines, typically with large windows to allow the maximum light in to aid with its operation and maintenance. Its walls were generally thick, often reinforced with shallow buttresses, stone plinths and deep foundations so it could provide support for the weight and movement of the heavy rocking beam and other moving parts. The pumps were usually housed in the basement, with the engines on the ground floor and the beams on the upper with a half floor between to provide access to the top of the cylinders. The designers of the engine house would also have to consider ventilation, so care was taken to provide openings in windows or louvred vents in the roof. They would also have to plan for the installation of the heavy cast-iron beams; in some cases these had to be hoisted into position before the building was complete.

OPPOSITE
This unique pumping station in Conyers Lane, Streatham Common, South London, was built in 1888. The main building has a rare circular plan with ornate Moorish domes and turrets.

Features from medieval castles can often be found on pumping stations. In this example from Stoke Newington, North London, the tallest tower was the chimney, the rear one a standpipe tower, and the pointed turret a staircase to access the roof.

The building attached to the engine house was the boiler room or house. Here a pair or series of horizontal boilers were installed to provide the steam to the cylinders next door. The walls would usually match the style of the engine house but could be less robust as they did not have to cope with the load and movement of the beam engines. Attached to this, or sited close by, was the coal store; this low building would sometimes have openings in the wall with chutes for the deliveries of coal. As the steam engines and pumps required constant maintenance and repair, most pumping stations

A glorious pumping station at Whitacre Waterworks, Shustoke, Warwickshire. Its church-like form, with a tall and narrow body, steep pitched roof and apsidal ends to the flanking buildings, is typical of the architectural style of the 1860s.

had workshops with a forge where parts could be made or repaired. There would also be stores for the tools required in the operation and cleaning of the machines and the other parts of the water supply and sewage disposal process.

With most pumping stations designed to be operational all year round, the superintendent and the men in charge of

This muscular engine house at Papplewick, Nottinghamshire, has buttresses in the form of pilasters to strengthen the structure, separate rows of windows illuminating the two main floors, and a louvred opening in the roof for ventilation.

Coleham Pumping Station, Shrewsbury, has its chimney, boiler and engine house arranged in a row. The engine house, which looks like a chapel, was built in 1901 as part of the town's new sewerage system.

keeping the machines running needed to be close at hand. Hence most sites had a fine house, often next to the entrance gates, for the man in charge, built in a style to complement the main building. Additional houses for the other key staff were set within the site or along the road leading up to the pumping

The maintenance workshop at Abbey Pumping Station, Leicester, had machinery for the repair and service of the engines and pumps. This was essential, as spare parts might not have been available at short notice if they broke down.

The superintendent of the pumping station would have had a fine house, usually near the entrance to the site. This example from Papplewick, Nottinghamshire, also features the original grand gates to the water works.

station. With very good accommodation and pleasant surroundings provided, working in a pumping station was a desirable job – although being tied to the site seven days a week would not have suited all.

The most prominent feature of the pumping station was the chimney. Its height was required for two reasons: firstly so that smoke from the boilers would dissipate in the air rather than just settle in the immediate area; and secondly to ensure that there was an uninterrupted draw of air into the boilers sufficient for the combustion

Chimneys and towers were often lavished with decorative brickwork and a bracketed sill, although few were as ornate as this example dating from 1881 at the former Bracebridge Pumping Station, Worksop, Nottinghamshire.

of the coal. The chimney could be attached directly to the boiler house or sited a short distance away and connected to them by underground flues. At Papplewick, Nottinghamshire, one large chimney was erected to remove the smoke from two separate boiler houses, although only one of these was eventually built. A protruding brick or masonry sill was fitted just below the top of the chimney to prevent the smoke simply pouring down the side of the shaft, and these were often the focus of decorative treatment.

Some chimneys were built in the form of a tower with a staircase inside to access the structure. Cleadon Tower in South Shields looks like a campanile (an Italian church bell tower), but was in fact a chimney for the old pumping station hidden in the trees below, with a staircase wrapped around the internal flue and a balcony at the top. Some towers had a different function: at London Museum of Water and Steam the imposing structure that dominates the site is a standpipe tower, which housed extensive pipework between the engines and the mains supply to absorb any fluctuations in pressure in the system. Unfortunately many chimneys have been removed – often because their cold north face is prone to its mortar

FAR LEFT
A Classical-style former pumping station in Perth, Scotland, built in the early 1830s. The stone rotunda is actually supported on a cast-iron framework and today houses the Fergusson Gallery.

LEFT
Leawood Pump House on the Cromford Canal, Derbyshire, was built in 1849 in a stout Classical style. Its large-capacity pump was necessary as water could only be taken from the River Derwent on one day each week.

being eroded by acids from condensing emissions on the inside, causing them to become unstable. At Abbey Mills in East London, however, the chimneys were demolished during the Second World War as it was feared that the huge stacks would be toppled by enemy bombs and damage the building below, disabling the city's sewerage system.

Many Victorian pumping stations, especially those built as part of drinking water supply and sewerage systems, are notable

A section of wall from Springhead Pumping Station, Hull, Yorkshire. The large round-arched windows, shallow pilasters and bracketed cornice have an Italianate flavour, popular in the 1850s and early 1860s.

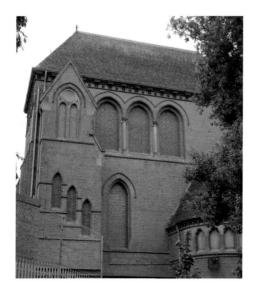

This former pumping station in Selly Oak, Birmingham, was built in a French Gothic style popular in the 1860s and '70s.

Circular corner turrets, battlements and Gothic pointed arches with colourful brickwork are typical of the 1870s but were rather outdated when this charming building at Bratch Pumping Station was opened in 1895.

for their extravagant style and ornate decoration. There are a number of reasons for this. These major works were often the earliest undertaken by the new local authorities. As the pumping station was the only visible part of the system it was the best opportunity for them to display their civic pride. Another driving force was competition; an imposing engine house and chimney built in the latest architectural style reflected the ambitions of a private company vying with rivals, or a local authority keen to outdo a neighbouring council. It was also important to have a stylish building in order to impress visiting dignitaries when they inspected these examples of groundbreaking engineering. The Victorians clad their buildings in historic styles not just because of the association with the past but also to reassure a wary public that the new technology they contained was safe and intended for the long term. Another reason for disguising the pumping station as an ancient structure at some sites was that the local aristocrat whose land it was built on did not wish his view spoilt. This obsession with the past meant that the engineers who designed the buildings had a vast palette of styles to

Ryhope Pumping Station, Sunderland, was designed by Thomas Hawksley and completed in 1869. The Dutch-style gables and cross windows are typical of the Jacobean Revival style.

choose from, and it also became acceptable to take a number of elements from different sources and create an eclectic style that was distinctive of a certain company or corporation.

Classical styles were still in vogue when Victoria came to the throne. Some pumping stations built for early water supply projects or to pump spa water were shaped like Ancient Greek or Roman temples. Even those erected for the mining industry and canal network could have a degree of elegance, with their plain walls divided up by pilasters, shallow columns built into the brickwork, and large, round-arched windows. A number of Victorian pumping stations were inspired by medieval castles,

Brindley Bank
Pumping
Station, Rugeley,
Staffordshire,
was designed
in-house by
the South
Staffordshire
Waterworks
Company in a
corporate style
using elements
of Tudor and
Jacobean
buildings.

with turrets and machicolations (the series of gaps between stone brackets under the battlements). Tudor buildings with red brick walls punctuated by stone rectangular windows and shallow arched doorways were a source of inspiration throughout the

This imposing
engine house at
Abbey Pumping
Station, Leicester,
designed in
1890 by leading
local architect
Stockdale
Harrison, was
intended to
resemble an
Elizabethan
mansion.

nineteenth century. By the late 1840s the Italianate style was becoming popular, based upon buildings from medieval and renaissance Italy. Low pitched, hipped slate roofs with a deep overhang supported on decorative brackets, rows of three or more round-arched openings or windows, and towers with shallow pyramidal roofs are distinctive of this style.

From the late 1850s the Gothic Revival began to compete with the Italianate in the design of corporate and public buildings. Roofs became steep pitched with patterned ridge tiles or intricate iron crests; walls were built with bands of differently coloured bricks or stone and prominent buttresses. Windows had pointed arches, and doors had elaborate stone surrounds and columns. Honesty in design was promoted so the openings in walls were positioned to reflect the use of the room behind; for instance, stairways were illuminated by small, stepped windows.

It was not long before many architects grew tired of the medieval Gothic and began to look at a wider range of historic sources for inspiration. Exotic styles based upon old buildings from around the Mediterranean coast and the British Empire were applied to a number of pumping stations. Tudor timber-framed houses and Dutch-style mansions from the late seventeenth century were the source for the Old English and Queen Anne styles which were used in some water and sewage works in the 1880s and '90s. Shaped gables, comprising curved and right-angled segments, and red terracotta mouldings and

This grand engine house built in 1912 on top of Bracebridge Heath Service Reservoir near Lincoln was designed in the Edwardian Baroque style.

tiles, were popular on these buildings. The Arts and Crafts Movement promoted the use of traditional materials, and areas of render or mock timber framing could be found on many buildings. By the turn of the twentieth century Classical styles once again became fashionable. Renaissance and Baroque-style buildings inspired new eclectic designs with wide segmental or elliptical arches, cream terracotta or white glazed tiles on the exterior, domed towers and extravagant moulded decoration.

This desire to break up wall surfaces with decorative patterns and elaborate mouldings was not restricted to the exterior of pumping stations. The huge iron columns and framework that helped support the weight of the beams were often cast as Classical or Gothic-style columns with richly decorated capitals. Glazed tiles were a practical and colourful surface for interior walls, and some windows were embellished with stained glass patterns and decorative ironwork fittings. In the finest restored examples the interior of the engine house is a breathtaking spectacle of colourful ironwork, polished brass and gleaming machinery.

OPPOSITE
The elaborate decorative metalwork applied to these huge cast-iron columns, which support the beam floor at Papplewick Pumping Station, Nottinghamshire, contains a variety of motifs and decorative details on a water theme.

A close-up of the stunning cast-iron work and colourful paint scheme around the octagonal well in the centre of the engine house at Crossness Pumping Station.

STEAM ENGINES, BOILERS AND PUMPS

THE STEAM ENGINE was the key component of the Victorian pumping station. Without their reliable power the vast water and sewerage schemes would not have been able to work. For some tasks one steam engine sufficed; in larger-scale operations there were usually a pair; and in the grandest schemes there could be four or more of these huge machines. The basic principles of a working steam engine to power a pump via a rocking overhead beam had been established during the eighteenth century by Thomas Newcomen and James Watt. Although there were further improvements made to these beam engines the priority for pumping stations was reliability and so they tended to grow in size and power rather than making great technological leaps during the Victorian period. It was not until the end of the nineteenth century that more efficient and powerful new types of steam engine began to displace the older beam engines, although many of the latter were still operating into the 1960s.

The steam-powered beam engines that were installed in most Victorian pumping stations were based upon the machine patented by Matthew Boulton and James Watt. It comprised a vertical cylinder with a piston inside, which was connected to a separate condenser. A series of valves let low pressure steam in one side of the piston and condensed that on the other side for the down stroke and then reciprocated the action the other way round to power the upstroke, making a double-acting or reciprocating engine. The rod running up

OPPOSITE
The beam, cylinders and ornate cast-iron columns at Abbey Pumping Station, Leicester, show the pride engineers had in these municipal works. The timber lagging around the cylinder provided insulation to reduce heat loss.

A reconstruction at the Black Country Living Museum, Birmingham, of Thomas Newcomen's first engine installed to pump water out of a local mine in Dudley.

A diagram of a Boulton and Watt double-acting steam engine. For clarity, the main water or sewage pump, which was normally connected to the end of the beam near the flywheel, is not shown.

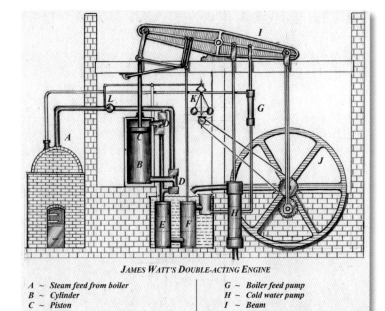

JAMES WATT'S DOUBLE-ACTING ENGINE

A	~	*Steam feed from boiler*	G	~	*Boiler feed pump*
B	~	*Cylinder*	H	~	*Cold water pump*
C	~	*Piston*	I	~	*Beam*
D	~	*Valves*	J	~	*Flywheel*
E	~	*Condenser*	K	~	*Governor*
F	~	*Condenser air pump*	L	~	*Throttle valve*

from the piston was connected to one end of the beam and moved it up and down. However, as the latter formed an arc when rocking Watt had to add a series of rods and bearings to keep the piston rod running on a true vertical line, which he called his 'parallel motion'. In most pumping stations the engines are described as 'rotative', whereby they had a large flywheel driven by a crank connected to the other end of the beam. This heavy wheel was fitted so its momentum smoothed out the jerky action of the beam engine and ensured the piston did not exceed its limits should the valves develop a fault.

There were further improvements made to the Boulton and Watt engine after the pair's patent had expired in 1800. Richard Trevithick introduced a machine that allowed high-pressure steam to be let in above the piston as the steam below it was condensed, but then the inlet valve was shut only part way through the stroke. Trevithick realised that high-pressure steam would continue to expand in the cylinder and used this to complete the stroke. By using a short burst of steam less coal was burnt in the boiler, making his Cornish engines popular in that county and other areas like London where the price of the fuel was high.

James Watt devised this governor to control the speed of the engine. If the flywheel were to spin faster, the rotating metal balls would swing further out, activating a rod that closed the steam inlet valve.

The operation of high-pressure engines was reliant upon the development of valves

Watt's parallel motion gear, the pivoted rods under the end of the beam in this view, were essential to keep the piston rod running in a vertical line.

The four cast-iron beams at Crossness Pumping Station with the currently unrestored pair in the foreground. Many beams had small oil cups on top of the bearings to keep them lubricated.

which could accurately control the release of steam and exhaust in a split second during a stroke. Most used double beat valves, also referred to as Cornish valves, which had two

A simplified drawing of a Woolf compound beam engine showing the main pump and air pressure vessel. The latter protected the system from fluctuations in water pressure.

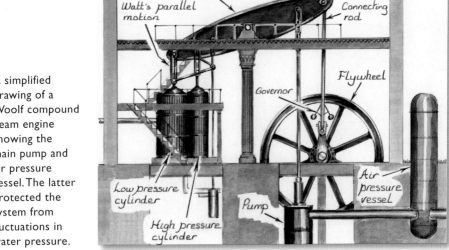

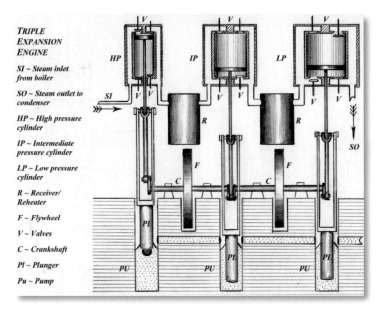

TRIPLE
EXPANSION
ENGINE

SI ~ Steam inlet
from boiler

SO ~ Steam outlet to
condenser

HP ~ High pressure
cylinder

IP ~ Intermediate
pressure cylinder

LP ~ Low pressure
cylinder

R ~ Receiver/
Reheater

F ~ Flywheel

V ~ Valves

C ~ Crankshaft

Pl ~ Plunger

Pu ~ Pump

A diagram of a
triple expansion
engine, showing
its key parts and
basic operation.

plugs in tandem; one was slightly larger than the other, so that
the steam acting on both would apply a fraction more pressure
upon the larger, which kept the valve shut but would only
require a small force to open it. These were usually mounted
together in valve chests and were opened and closed in a set
timing pattern by cams and rods connected to the flywheel or
beam. Long levers were used to open and close them manually
when starting the engine up before its momentum took over.

In a single cylinder the high-pressure steam cooled as it
expanded; this resulted in the repeated heating and cooling of
the cylinder, which was inefficient. Another Cornish engineer,
Arthur Woolf, realised that the steam exhausted from this
cylinder was at the same pressure as that which entered a
Watt engine. He patented a compound steam engine which
had a second larger, low-pressure cylinder connected to the
smaller high-pressure vessel. The exhausted low-pressure
steam applied roughly the same force on the large piston as
the high-pressure steam did on the smaller piston, so both
cylinders would produce roughly equal power. By allowing

The huge triple expansion engine at Kempton Steam Museum, London.

A Cornish boiler with a single flue running through the length of the cylindrical vessel. The Y-shaped piece on top is part of the safety valve mechanism, which originally had a pair of weighted levers on top.

the expansion of steam to take place in the two cylinders of a compound engine the heat loss was reduced, which improved its efficiency; moreover, if one cylinder failed the machine could still carry on operating on the other.

The engineers of Victorian pumping stations were still installing these reliable beam engines even after more modern and compact steam engines had been adopted in other industries. This was mainly because coal was plentiful and cheap, the engines had a very long life and the technology was proven to be reliable, an essential consideration for machines which had to be able to provide power every day of the year. However, by the 1890s beam engines began to be superseded by horizontal engines in smaller works and new triple expansion steam engines in larger pumping stations.

A row of Lancashire boilers at Papplewick Pumping Station, with water level sight glasses and pressure gauges on the front above the fire doors and a safety valve on the top.

The latter had three cylinders rather than the two of Woolf's compound engine, with an intermediate between the low- and high-pressure vessels. These cylinders were arranged in a row and were inverted so their piston rods ran down to the pumps below, to drive them directly, rather than to a beam above. A pair of flywheels were fitted at right angles between the cylinders. The triple arrangement and the connection of the three piston rods to the crankshaft at points 120 degrees to each other produced a smooth and reliable delivery of power.

The design of the boilers, which provided steam to the engines, had also evolved to improve efficiency and create steam at higher pressures. Watt's engines used wagon boilers with an external fire heating the metal tank of water to produce steam at a pressure of around 5–10lb psi. Trevithick needed much higher pressures and thanks to developments in wrought-iron production and new methods of riveting around the turn of the nineteenth century he was able to create his Cornish boiler. It had a horizontal cylindrical body, which Trevithick realised was the best shape to resist the pressure, with a large single fire tube running through the lower half. Hot gasses from the combustion chamber at the front of the boiler would pass along this tube, heating the water before returning through channels in the brickwork casing up the side and under the base to maximise the efficiency of the boiler. These Cornish boilers could produce steam at around 50lb psi.

Boiler explosions were a concern, so a lever safety valve was fitted at the top of boilers. These had a hinged arm holding the valve in place with a sliding weight on the far end, which could be adjusted to release the steam if the pressure became excessive. Problems continued, however, often caused by low water levels in the boiler, so William Fairbairn, an expert in the study and manufacture of metal structures, devised the Lancashire boiler. This had two smaller diameter fire tubes, which together provided a greater heating surface area than a single tube but were under less strain and could be covered by a greater depth of water, reducing the chance of explosion. In 1851 W & J Galloway introduced their own boiler based upon the Lancashire but with the two flues joining part-way down the boiler to form a single flat-topped vessel with conical stays, which allowed water to pass through, improving the circulation of water within the boiler. There were further improvements made, including reinforcing rings around the tubes and the use of steel, which improved safety at higher pressures. As a result, Lancashire boilers were still being installed in pumping stations into the early twentieth century.

Another advance that further increased the efficiency of boilers was Edward Green's economiser, patented in 1845. This ran the cold

A diagram showing the basic operation of a lift pump with a piston (left) and a force pump with a plunger (right). The latter had the advantage: they did not need a machined cylinder and had fewer issues with matter in the water clogging the seal around the top.

LIFT PUMP   PLUNGER PUMP

S ~ Seal   V ~ Flap valve
P ~ Piston   I ~ Water inlet
Pl ~ Plunger   O ~ Water outlet

water feed to the boiler through the hot gases exhausted from it and thus increased the temperature of the water entering the boiler, saving money on coal and reducing the heat of the exhaust up the chimney. Firing of the boiler was also critical to efficient and safe running; since manual labour was not always reliable, mechanical stokers were introduced from the 1820s and incorporated in some larger pumping stations.

The main pumps powered by the engines were usually sited below the floor of the engine house but were sometimes partially visible in the basement. Most of the pumps used in the water supply and sewage industry were either piston or plunger pumps. The former had a piston with a seal around its edge fitted within a cylinder and could work either as a lift or force pump. In a lift pump the piston had valves in it, so when it was pulled up it drew in water from below and then, as it pushed down, the water trapped in the bottom of the cylinder passed through the piston valves into the upper section of the cylinder. As the piston was pulled up again the water in the upper section was forced out through a pipe at the top of the cylinder as the next batch of water was sucked up from below. In a force pump the piston draws up the water into the cylinder; then, as it is pushed down on the power stroke from the beam engine, it ejects this water through an outlet to the side. Plunger pumps are a type of force pump, but rather than having a tightly fitted piston they use a large metal plunger which forces the water out by displacement. These were able to work with higher pressures and their seals were not worn by matter in the liquid; hence, they were especially popular in the sewage industry. Other smaller air and water pumps were also used in the operation of the steam engine, usually powered by rods connected to the beam. Steam-powered centrifugal pumps, with a shell-shaped casing and a rotating impeller inside which drove the fluid along, were introduced in the 1850s and were in widespread use by the early twentieth century.

WATER WORKS

CREATING A RELIABLE and clean source of water for major towns and cities had been a problem for centuries. There had been various schemes since medieval times to supply water into London, including the New River Company, which opened its 39-mile channel bringing spring water from Hertfordshire to Islington in 1613. However, as the population began to grow in the second half of the eighteenth century, existing sources like this proved inadequate so new private companies were established, many of which drew water from the River Thames. One of these, the Chelsea Waterworks Company, was supplying the Royal Palaces when, after a severe water shortage in 1739, they were forced to install a Newcomen steam engine to improve supply; this was the first steam pumping station built to supply drinking water.

As the River Thames became polluted complaints from customers arose about the poor quality of the water, especially that from the Chelsea Waterworks Company. In 1829 they employed James Simpson to build the first slow sand filtration system for a public water supply, a concept first devised by John Gibb for his bleachery in Paisley, Scotland. Water from the river was passed through a thick bed of fine sand on top of which a thin biological film formed which carried out the purification process. The success of Simpson's filter system encouraged others to copy and develop it around the country.

Another important step was made by a young self-taught engineer, Thomas Hawksley. In 1832 his Trent Waterworks in

OPPOSITE
The former pumping station at Hatton, Staffordshire, which began supplying water in 1892 from boreholes below the site. It has now been converted into luxury housing.

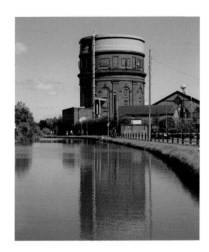

Nottingham were opened, where a supply from the river was filtered and pumped by steam engine to a reservoir. Previously water was supplied intermittently so fluids could potentially enter the pipework but in Hawksley's new system the water was run through cast-iron pipes with the feed under constant pressure; this prevented contaminants leaking into the system. His design was slowly adopted elsewhere and Hawksley became the leading engineer for waterworks and pumping stations across the country.

Despite the availability of the technology to pump and filter water, many areas were still putting up with a poor-quality supply. Water might contain pollutants, the supply might only run for a few hours a day, and the low pressure of many systems meant taps could only work on the ground floor of houses. The problem in many areas was that water was supplied by numerous small private companies, who did not have the funds to invest in new pumping stations, reservoirs and dams. As a result it was not until new legislation was introduced from the late 1840s that the municipal authorities began buying them out in some towns and cities and investing in new, large-scale projects. In Liverpool powers granted in 1847 enabled the city corporation to purchase existing private companies and improve the public water supply, which included providing public baths and drinking fountains. Other towns and cities followed suit, at first mainly across the North and Midlands and only later over the whole country. Despite this, in a few urban areas including Portsmouth, Cambridge, Bristol and South Staffordshire, the private companies established in this period are still supplying water today.

Problems persisted in London: the numerous private companies had agreed in 1811 to keep to their geographical area, thus removing much of their competitive drive and restricting investment during the Victorian period. The Grand Junction Water Works Company was formed when the canal company of the same name realised it could supply drinking water to London from its canals and reservoirs. This proved inadequate and of poor quality so they built a pumping station at Chelsea to take water from the River Thames. Complaints about the water persisted so they moved their supply further upstream, hoping to find less polluted water at Kew Bridge, opening a new pumping station there in 1838. The old Boulton and Watt engines from the Chelsea works were moved to Kew, a new 90-inch cylinder Cornish engine was installed, and reservoirs were created on the site during the 1840s. However, the 1852 Metropolis Water Act forced the company to source its supply from a non-tidal stretch of the Thames so a new pumping station was built upstream at Hampton, and the Kew Bridge site became an intermediate waterworks with an even larger 100-foot Cornish engine added in 1871. As these engines did not have flywheels their action

The former Stoke Newington Pumping Station, London, was inspired by medieval castles with the letters of the surname of its creator William Chadwell Mylne and the date of construction carved onto the buttresses. It now houses a climbing centre.

The chimney tower at the former Bestwood Pumping Station, Nottinghamshire, which has been restored as a restaurant and spa.

created a pulsed supply, so a large standpipe tower was erected with vertical cast-iron pipes to absorb these fluctuations and protect the engines if there was a leak further down in the system. The original standpipe tower was damaged by frost in 1867 so a new, 200-foot-high tower was erected, this time encased in brick, with space for fires to be lit at the base in extreme cold weather.

The Metropolis Water Act also forced companies in London to filter their supplies and cover certain channels along their networks. The New River Company, which had been supplying its spring water for over two hundred years, was forced to cover its channel on the approach to the City, and although its waters were cleaner than most it still had to be purified to comply with the legislation. Filter beds were built in Stoke Newington and a large pumping station erected there to pump the cleansed water through cast-iron pipes to a huge underground reservoir in Claremont Square, Pentonville. The new pumping station was designed like a Scottish castle (its architect, R. W. Billings, was an expert on Scottish architecture and the engineer William Chadwell Mylne was of Scottish lineage). Inside were six Boulton and Watt steam engines supplied by eighteen boilers, with flywheels weighing 35 tons each and protruding out of the building, with the buttresses covering their outer edge. It was not until 1902 that these private water companies in London were taken over and the Metropolitan Water Board established, so larger-scale projects could be planned.

In Nottingham industrial growth around the cloth industry had been rapid and pollution in the river water had become an issue. In 1845 the existing small water companies were amalgamated into the Nottingham Waterworks Company, with Thomas Hawksley as its engineer. He created new supplies of clean water from wells dug into the porous sandstone under the north of the city. A new pumping station was built at the Park Works at the top of The Ropewalk, with additional ones added at Bagthorpe in 1857 and Bestwood in 1871. The old company was taken over by the Nottingham Corporation in 1880 and they sought to increase supply as demand continued to grow. Their engineer, Marriott Ogle Tarbotton, had test boreholes dug at a site near the village of Papplewick, north of Nottingham, where Hawksley had already built a reservoir. With successful results, a large pumping station was planned with two engine and boiler houses served by a tall single chimney, although ultimately only one set of buildings was completed. Inside these were two 140hp rotative steam engines supplied by James Watt and Co., whilst steam was supplied by a row of six Lancashire boilers from the Galloway Company. The engines pumped water out of the 200-foot-deep well and up a further 130 feet into Hawksley's reservoir, which supplied it under gravity to Nottingham. Usually only one engine would be working at a time but on Mondays both often had to be used; as factories had been closed over the weekend the air was relatively clean so Monday was the best day for housewives to wash and hang out the laundry, causing an increased demand for water.

Thomas Hawksley was involved in numerous other schemes across the

Ryhope Pumping Station, Sunderland, continued to pump water until 1967; it has now been restored to full working order. The pond in the foreground was not ornamental but supplied cold water to the steam engines.

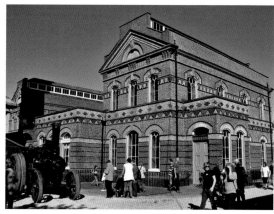

ABOVE LEFT
Dalton Pumping
Station was
designed
by Thomas
Hawksley for the
Sunderland and
South Shields
Water Company
and used Cornish
engines due to
the great depth
of the well.

ABOVE RIGHT
The former
Goldstone
Waterworks in
Brighton is now
the site of British
Engineerium, an
engineering and
steam power
museum in West
Blatchington,
Hove.

country, including that run by the Sunderland and South Shields Water Company, formed in 1852. As their engineer he designed new pumping stations at Fulwell and Cleadon, the latter with its chimney disguised as a 100-foot campanile that still dominates the landscape around South Shields. In 1864 the company purchased land at Ryhope, Sunderland; a new pumping station was planned by Hawksley to extract naturally filtered water from the limestone below the area. As was the case in many engine houses, the huge size of the machinery meant the engine and building had to be erected simultaneously, with the beams craned in before the roof was added. The pair of rotative compound steam engines was supplied by R & W Hawthorn of Newcastle, each with a 22-ton beam and 18-ton flywheel, helping extract over 40,000 gallons of water each hour from the 250-foot-deep wells for over a hundred years.

Another project Hawksley advised upon was in Brighton, where the growing seaside town and its neighbours took their water from wells dug into the natural aquifer in the chalk rocks but now needed a more reliable supply. The first company set up to offer an improved service only managed to provide a couple of hours of water to select customers and were bought out in 1854 by a new venture, The Brighton,

Hove and Preston Constant Water Service Company. They asked Hawksley to advise them where to establish a new pumping station and in 1866 they built a new works on the site he identified at Goldstone, near Hove. When the company was bought out by Brighton Corporation six years later they were already pumping over 2.5 million gallons every day to around 18,000 customers. The original Woolf compound engine built by Easton and Amos provided 120hp but a second, more powerful model was added in a new engine house alongside the original in 1876. The building, now the site of British Engineerium, has bands and patterns formed by differently coloured bricks, making a striking impact typical of the 1860s, with an impressive muscular chimney rising to nearly 100 feet.

Hawksley's son Charles became a partner in his business and took over T & C Hawksley upon his father's death in 1893. One of the major schemes he was involved in was for the Bristol Waterworks Company, which had been established in 1846 after seeing off a rival bid backed by Isambard Kingdom Brunel. They employed Charles Hawksley to help design a new

BELOW LEFT
Tees Cottage Pumping Station has a pair of red domed cylinders which are air pressure vessels designed to protect the mains and engines from fluctuation in supply.

BELOW RIGHT
Pipe Hill Pumping Station, near Lichfield, was completed in 1907 and housed a pair of horizontal compound steam engines.

reservoir, dam and pumping station at Blagdon on the edge of the Mendip Hills to supply water into the city. The scheme was large enough to justify the Great Western Railway building a new line to the site, firstly to supply building materials during construction and secondly coal for the steam engines after its completion in 1905. The engine houses were built in a restrained Jacobean style with a pair of Woolf compound steam engines in each – possibly the last beam engines installed in a waterworks in Britain. The chimney sited between them was in the form of a large Gothic tower but it was truncated after electric pumps replaced steam, so only the lower section survives. Bristol Waterworks Company (known today simply as Bristol Water) is one of the few water supply companies that has remained in private ownership since its foundation.

Away from the major cities there were many smaller but vital projects to supply water to towns that still required their own pumping stations. The piecemeal development of these local waterworks can best be seen at the former Broomy Hill Waterworks in Hereford. It started life as a single beam engine and boiler house in 1856, pumping water from the river below to a small reservoir on the hill above. As demand increased and the urban area expanded, so new engine and boiler houses were added alongside the original, including one of the earliest installations of a triple expansion steam engine at a waterworks in 1895. A new water tower was also added above the waterworks to gain height so there would be sufficient pressure to supply new houses being built around Broomy Hill. Today the site is the Waterworks Museum and the numerous gables of the

Sandfields Pumping Station, Lichfield, was built in local blue brick and was completed in 1873. It still houses its original Cornish engine, which the Lichfield Waterworks Trust is working to restore and open to the public.

Springhead Pumping Station in Hull was built in 1863 in an Italianate style with its staircase tower topped by a lantern. The taller building to the rear was added in 1876.

Classically styled façade record each new addition made to the works during the second half of the nineteenth century.

Cropston Pumping Station and the adjoining reservoir were built in the 1870s to supply water into Leicester. It is now a restaurant and function venue.

SEWAGE WORKS

SYSTEMS FOR REMOVING sewage from buildings in Britain have been found dating as far back as Roman times. Medieval monks diverted river water through drains under their abbeys to maintain cleanliness. Most urban areas in Britain had no such luxuries: human waste was generally collected in cesspits and pools or run off directly into local streams and rivers. These crude methods first became a problem in London, where legislation to control sewage was introduced in the Tudor period. As the population of major towns and cities grew and water closets began to be installed during the early nineteenth century, piecemeal networks of sewers were built and local legislation introduced to try to improve the disposal of human waste. With the spread of disease being increasingly linked to the pollution of watercourses, from the 1850s the authorities began to invest money in new sewer networks. As these would rely upon gravity, pumping stations would be required to raise the waste water at certain points to maintain a flow along its route.

In these early sewerage systems the waste water was usually dumped into a section of river or sea which was far enough out so as not to flow back into the urban area. It was soon recognised that this was only passing the problem further downstream. The Rivers Pollution Act of 1876 sought to restrict the dumping of raw sewage into rivers, mainly to reduce the build-up of the river bed and to protect fish stocks; however, most places found a way around the regulations.

OPPOSITE
The former Bracebridge Pumping Station at Worksop, Nottinghamshire, was built in 1881 as part of the town's new sewerage system. Coal was brought to the site from a local colliery via the Chesterfield Canal, shown in the foreground.

It was not until the following decade that treatment works began to be installed in which the sewage was passed through grids, settlement tanks and filter beds; the sludge collected was often passed onto farmers as fertiliser. In the early twentieth century the aeration process – in which bacteria are used to further purify the waste water – was introduced.

The scale of the problem in London was huge. There was a complex arrangement of existing sewers and old rivers flowing into the Thames from both the north and south. New legislation in the 1830s and '40s had ensured that not only waste water from houses but also any existing cesspools were connected to the sewers, increasing the quantities of effluent flowing into the Thames. In 1856 Joseph Bazalgette, the Chief Engineer for the new Metropolitan Board of Works, put forward his ambitious plans for a massive sewerage system. On both the north and south side of the city three levels of sewers would run west to east, collecting the effluent from existing sewers and using the rainwater and waste water collected in drains to help dilute it and wash it along for disposal into the river far beyond the city limits. While the plans were debated

The colourful Gothic Revival-style walls of Abbey Mills Pumping Station, East London. Although it is rarely open to the public it can be viewed from the Greenway footpath, which runs along the top of the Northern Outfall Sewer.

and amended, a particularly hot and dry summer in 1858 meant water levels dropped and sewage was left on the dry bed of the River Thames, causing such a foul odour that the press labelled it 'The Great Stink'. This literally got right up the noses of MPs sitting in the Houses of Parliament and they passed legislation granting the Metropolitan Board of Works the power to build Bazalgette's sewerage system and borrow £3 million, which could be paid back through a three-penny levy on all households in London.

This vast project took over fifteen years to complete and included building the Victoria, Albert and Chelsea Embankments, under which would run the low-level intercepting sewer as well as a new underground railway topped by a road to help relieve traffic congestion. The gradient was sufficient for gravity to move the waste water down the pipes, but additional pumping stations were required to raise the water up into a higher section to keep the flow going. To the north the low-level sewer was raised by around 18 feet at the Western Pumping Station on Grosvenor Street; this had four 90hp beam engines, each operating two plunger pumps. Where the three intercepting sewers met in the east of the city another large pumping station was built at Abbey Mills to lift the waste from the lower one into the outfall from the middle and upper pipes. This was the architectural showpiece of the system, with an elaborate and colourful exterior and a cruciform plan housing a pair of steam engines in each arm. From here the Northern Outfall Sewer carried the combined waste down to Beckton where it was stored in large holding reservoirs and then released just after high tide twice a day so it would be carried out to sea.

The three main southern sewers met at Deptford, where another pumping station was built to lift the lower one to the height of the others. From here the waste travelled along the Southern Outfall Sewer until it reached the River Thames at Crossness, where Bazalgette built another pumping

Abbey Pumping Station, Leicester, which first started pumping in 1890, still retains its original four beam engines with their elaborate cast-iron decoration. It is open daily to the public.

station to lift it into the holding reservoirs for the twice-daily disposal into the tidal river. Four huge single-cylinder beam engines were built by James Watt and Co. to the engineers' specification, each providing 125hp with 43-foot iron beams and flywheels weighing over 50 tons. Steam was provided by twelve Cornish boilers, which consumed around 5,000 tons of coal each year. The engines operated a series of plunger pumps below the floor, each of which could shift 6 tons of fluid per stroke.

The disposal of raw sewage into the tidal river was to have tragic consequences only a few years after Bazalgette's system was complete. In September 1878 the *Princess Alice* steamship sank after colliding with another craft in the River Thames close to Crossness, claiming the lives of over 650 people. It was believed in the aftermath that the twice-daily release of 75 million gallons of raw sewage from the pumping stations had contributed to the high death rate, as the bodies had risen to the surface much more quickly than would be expected, implying they had consumed some of the waste. In 1882 a Royal Commission recommended that the solid mater should be separated out of the sewage, and in 1891 sedimentation tanks were added, with the sludge carried away in boats to be dumped further out at sea.

The adoption of water closets in other parts of the country in the mid-nineteenth century was slow, as in many areas there was not an adequate water supply to flush toilets or a system of sewers that could cope with the additional load. As the existing systems of cesspits linked into sewers or rivers proved inadequate, many authorities introduced dry methods of removing human waste, using metal pails, brick-lined middens and earth closets. In Manchester during the late 1870s the local authority cleared out all the old dunghills and cesspits, disconnected them from the sewers and introduced metal pails or brick-lined middens in order to reduce the pressure on its sewerage system.

In Leicester the authorities also installed thousands of metal pails for poorer families, but the system of removal was expensive and pollution still found its way into the local river. In 1886 they decided to build a new sewage farm outside the urban area at Beaumont Leys to deal with the problem. Abbey Pumping Station was built down by the river to raise the waste uphill to the new works. It was designed by Stockdale Harrison, a local architect, to resemble an Elizabethan mansion, with four compound rotative beam engines supplied by Gimson and Co. who were based in the city.

Claymills Pumping Station in Burton upon Trent, with its impressive muscular buildings dating from the 1880s, has regular public steamings.

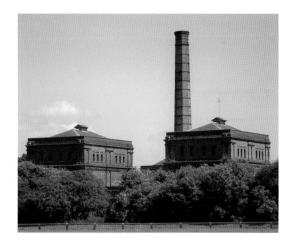

A short distance away at Burton upon Trent there was an additional problem. The town was the centre of the brewing industry and huge quantities of foul waste product was poured into streams; this, combined with the local effluent, caused pollution and an offending stench in the River Trent which flowed through the town. The local authorities built a sewer to collect the waste and send it outside of the urban area to a site called Claymills where it could be discharged into the river. This merely passed the problem a few miles downstream so in 1880 the Burton upon Trent Corporation obtained an act of Parliament to build a new sewage farm a few miles away on higher ground where the waste would be processed, and to erect a pumping station on the Claymills site to pump the raw sewage to it. Two engine houses were built either side of a central boiler house and chimney with a pair of Woolf compound rotative beam engines in each one, supplied by Gimson and Co. of Leicester. The beams are interesting in that rather than being cast iron they are made from wrought-iron sheets riveted together to form a box girder, which makes for a much lighter construction. A row of Lancashire boilers supplied steam to the engines, which could pump over 5 million gallons a day.

Portsmouth had a more acute problem with sewage than most other Victorian towns, as the urban area was relatively flat and in places just over 10 feet above the surrounding sea level. Waste could easily contaminate the water supply and in 1849 around 670 people died from cholera. The local authority completed the first sewers in 1868; these drained the waste by gravity down to Eastney, where a pumping station was built to raise it back up to a level so it could be let out into Langstone Harbour just after high tide. The authorities later ensured that any property within 100 yards of the new sewer had to connect up to it but they soon found that the pumping station was overwhelmed and the pipes were becoming blocked. They set about improving the facilities and built large holding tanks to contain the waste until it was ready to be released and erected a new pumping station in 1887 adjacent to the original one, this time with two more powerful 150hp James Watt and Co. beam engines.

Despite Cambridge having the image of an elegant university city in the mid-nineteenth century, it had areas of slum housing with unsanitary conditions made all the worse by a lack of proper drainage. The need for a sewer system was appreciated from an early date as the River Cam became polluted, but little was done until 1895 when deep underground sewers were completed to collect the waste and direct it to a site north of the town where a new pumping station dispatched it to a treatment works at nearby Milton. The engines were Hathorn Davey compound engines, but rather than having a large beam overhead the cylinders were mounted horizontally and were connected to a rocking disc which raised and lowered the vertical pump rods. The steam was provided by three destructor boilers, which burnt household rubbish rather than coal, but these were supplemented at a later date by an additional coke-fed boiler.

Cheddars Lane Pumping Station in Cambridge is now the Museum of Technology. Unusually the taller building is the boiler house, with the horizontal steam engines installed in the low building in the centre.

MINES, LAND DRAINAGE AND HYDRAULIC POWER

THE DEPTH TO which mine shafts could be dug was restricted by flooding as water seeping out of the rock filled the workings. Pumps driven by manual labour or animals were used at some sites; at others miners dug sloughs, narrow tunnels with a slight gradient, which drained the water out into a lower watercourse. At Wanlockhead, in Dumfries and Galloway, Scotland, is situated a unique water-powered beam engine dating from the mid-nineteenth century. It has a pivoted beam with one end connected to a pump rod and the other to a suspended bucket, filled by the nearby stream. As the bucket fills, it tilts the beam over, lifting the pump rod. The bucket then empties and the weight of the pump rod tilts the beam back the other way and the bucket begins refilling to start the procedure again.

The introduction of the steam engine connected by rods to a series of pumps running down the shaft enabled mines to be dug hundreds of feet deep. Engine houses were erected by mine owners to drain single or multiple mines, with most dating from the late eighteenth or nineteenth century. They tend to be simple in design with plain, robust chimneys. At Elsecar, near Barnsley, a Newcomen engine was installed in 1795 to enable deeper mining of the coal seams and is the oldest steam pumping engine still in its original location. In 1820 the Levant Mining Company was formed to develop a tin and copper mine on a clifftop site near St Just, Cornwall. A steam pumping engine was installed in 1840 and enabled the workings to

OPPOSITE
The shell of Windmill End Pumping Station, Rowley Regis, West Midlands, which was erected in 1831 to pump water out of local mines. Its steam engine was moved to the Henry Ford Museum, Dearborn, Michigan, in 1930.

Dog Dyke Steam Drainage Station near Tattershall, Lincolnshire, was built in 1856 to replace an old wind pump. It still contains its original beam engine and scoop wheel, which are regularly in action.

extend out over a mile under the sea and this building has now been restored by the National Trust.

The Levant Mine engine had been supplied by Harvey and Co. of Hayle, Cornwall, one of the leading manufacturers of stationary steam engines for the mining industry. Its founder John Harvey had developed his Cornish engines with Richard Trevithick, who had married his daughter, and his son Henry, who continued the business, employed Arthur Woolf as engineer. Harvey and Co. also built what is probably the largest steam engine in the world, used from 1850 to drain Haarlemmermeer, west of Amsterdam, Holland. It has a huge single cylinder over 3.5m in diameter in the centre of a round tower, which powered a series of radiating beams protruding through the walls to pumps set around the exterior. This massive pumping station was one of three, which emptied the lake in just over three years. The unique building is preserved as the Cruquius Museum.

Ever since the early seventeenth century private drainage schemes were undertaken to convert large areas of seasonally flooded land into fields for agriculture, most notably in the Fens. The networks of straight drains and rivers were initially successful in drying out the soil but the deep layers of peat that covered many of these areas began to shrink and decompose while loose soil was also blown away. As a result the ground level in the Fens began to drop and flooding once again became a problem. Wind-powered pumps were used to raise water from the fields up into the main drainage rivers which were now at a higher level. These operated a scoop wheel, which had angled paddles to lift up water from a lower channel and deposit it in the upper one.

These wind pumps had limited capacity and could not operate when the conditions were still; hence the full agricultural potential of the Fens and other low-lying areas was not achieved until steam-powered pumps were introduced from the 1820s. These provided a more reliable and rapid rate of drainage. Around a hundred steam-powered pumping engines were installed over the Fens in the nineteenth century, replacing eight times as many wind-powered pumps. However, every time the drainage became more efficient the land dropped again and a new, larger diameter scoop wheel or more powerful machine had to be installed. In the twentieth century these were replaced by diesel engines or electric motors connected to more effective centrifugal pumps and today there are over 280 of these pumping stations in the Fens.

Pinchbeck Engine near Spalding, Lincolnshire, could only produce 20hp but still managed to lift between around 1 and 3.5 million tons of water each year.

Stretham Old Engine, Cambridgeshire, was built in 1831 by Butterleys of Derby, who provided the mechanical equipment and erected the building.

Westonzoyland Pumping Station, near Bridgwater, Somerset, not only has its original Easton and Amos engine but also a fine collection of other steam engines within this popular heritage site.

Despite some early drainage systems being dug on the Somerset Levels, wind-powered pumps seem rarely to have been used here. The first steam-powered pumping station was built at Westonzoyland in 1830, with a beam engine operating a scoop wheel which lifted water from a drainage channel known as a 'rhyne' (pronounced *reen*) up into the River Parrett. However, as the land sank around it the wheel became ineffective and was replaced by an Easton and Amos engine with a new centrifugal pump thirty years later. The success of this machine resulted in similar machines being established across the Levels.

Although these rural pumping stations were smaller than most urban types, they still required the same buildings and machinery along with accommodation for the men who operated it. Coal was consumed in copious quantities and in most cases it would have been brought by barge along the rivers and drains they served. At Pinchbeck Pumping Station near Spalding a narrow gauge railway was built from the local line with coal wagons pushed by hand along the route to the engine house. At Westonzoyland accommodation was added in the 1860s for the station keeper, with a forge on site where he could make and repair tools. At Stretham, Cambridgeshire, one of the keepers had a telescope installed in his cottage next door to the pumping station so he could keep an eye on his men.

Pumping stations were also built along the summit levels of canals and at docks, where they were separated from tidal waters by a lock. Every time a boat passed through a lock it would drain water from the higher level, so steam-powered pumps were used to return it into the summit or dock. At

Claverton on the Kennet and Avon Canal which opened in 1810, a waterwheel powered by the neighbouring River Avon drove a pair of cast-iron beams and pumps which could deliver nearly 100,000 gallons an hour into the waterway. Around the same time at Crofton steam was used to power the pumps, which filled the summit level of the same canal. One of the two beam engines at this pumping station is the oldest working example; it is still performing its original task on the same site after 200 years. In Birmingham the Old Main Line Canal had a pumping station with an early James Watt engine built in 1779 at Smethwick to top up the summit level. This was replaced by a new pumping station in 1892 with the latest compound engine powering centrifugal pumps. The original Watt engine was saved and is now in Thinktank, Birmingham, and is currently the oldest working steam engine in the world.

New Smethwick Pumping Station was built in 1892 to raise water between Birmingham's Main Line Canals. It has been restored and is now the home of the Galton Valley Canal Heritage Centre.

Victorian pumping stations were also built to provide hydraulic power. Some heavy machinery and lifting gear were required intermittently, especially in docks where cranes, lock gates and lift bridges were only used when boats arrived and could remain stationary for large parts of the day. Keeping a steam engine constantly fired up on standby for occasional use was very inefficient. The answer was hydraulic power, a constant high-pressure water supply which could be turned on and off when required. Joseph Bramah, who invented the hydraulic press and manufactured water closets, was the first to see the potential of a hydraulic system – as early as 1812 – but it was William Armstrong, a solicitor and part-time inventor

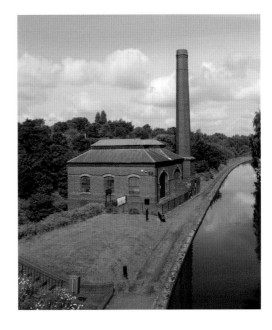

The former Central Hydraulic Tower and Pumping Station, Birkenhead. Its 110-foot accumulator tower was based upon the Palazzo Vecchio in Florence and was completed in 1863 although it lost its upper stage during Second World War bombing.

from Newcastle, who made the first practical application. In 1845 the local water company was laying on a new mains supply to the city and Armstrong used the excess pressure down by the river to power his first hydraulic crane. This greatly increased the speed of operation and orders for more followed such that he quit his law practice and built a factory by the Tyne from which he could manufacture his hydraulic machinery and supply it around the country. Initially if there was not an adequate water supply on the site Armstrong would build a tall tower with a tank at the top to provide constant pressurised water for the machinery. The most notable of these is the huge Grimsby Dock Tower, one of a pair that provided a head of water to operate the lock gates. Such a huge structure was costly and could not always be built if the ground was unsuitable, so in 1850 Armstrong developed an idea first suggested by Bramah: the accumulator – a vertical metal cylinder with a water inlet and outlet at the bottom and a large piston inserted above with a very heavy weight on top. A steam engine was used to pump water into the system so the piston would rise in the accumulator until the cylinder was full and would then provide the necessary pressurised water when required. Hydraulic machinery was installed at docks and other works across the country, with a pumping station and accumulator tower providing the pressurised water through cast-iron pipes.

Bramah had envisaged a public hydraulic system working off a ring main and in 1876 the first such system was installed in Hull. Companies could take a feed off the system to power their machinery for a fee and similar networks were installed in London, Manchester, Liverpool, Glasgow, and Birmingham.

The London Hydraulic Company established in 1884 used five pumping stations to provide pressurised water through over 180 miles of cast-iron pipework to factories, docks and even curtain-raising machinery in the theatres. A separate hydraulic system was also installed in Tower Bridge to lift the bascules; two of the accumulators and the old pumping station still stand on the southern end of the bridge. These Victorian systems were used until the Second World War, but bomb damage crippled many of them and they were superseded by electricity shortly afterwards. The London system continued to be used into the late 1970s when its pipework was bought out by a telecommunications company to lay down its fibre optic network under the city.

PLACES TO VISIT

Abbey Pumping Station, Corporation Road,
    Leicester LE4 5PX. Telephone: 0116 299 5111.
    Website: www.abbeypumpingstation.org *Excellent
    pumping station with four restored beam engines and
    displays outlining how water and sewerage systems work. It
    also contains Leicester's Museum of Science and Technology
    and is next door to the National Space Centre.*
Black Country Living Museum, Tipton Road,
    Dudley DY1 4SQ. Telephone: 0121 557 9643.
    Website: www.bclm.co.uk *This vast museum is a must for
    anyone interested in life and industry in the Victorian period.
    It also features a working reconstruction of a Newcomen
    engine that was built close by to pump out the local mines.*
British Engineerium, The Droveway, Hove, East
    Sussex BN3 7QA. Telephone: 01273 554070.
    Website: www.britishengineerium.org *Colourful historic
    buildings and working steam engines form the heart of this
    Victorian pumping station.*

Cambridge Museum of Technology, The Old Pumping Station, Cheddars Lane, Cambridge CB5 8LD. Telephone: 01223 368650. Website: www.museumoftechnology.com *A fascinating museum next to the River Cam with a pair of Hathorn Davey pumping engines driving a rocking disc and many other displays.*

Claymills Pumping Station, Meadow Lane, Stretton, Burton on Trent, Staffordshire DE13 0DA. Telephone: 01283 509929. Website: www.claymills.org.uk *Impressive pumping station with restored beam engines, pumps and many other artefacts from the site.*

Coleham Pumping Station, Longden Coleham, Shrewsbury SY3 7DN. Telephone: 01743 362947. Website: www.colehampumpingstation.co.uk *Very attractive small pumping station beside the River Severn with its original beam engines and boilers.*

Cornish Mines and Engines, Agar Road, Pool, Redruth TR15 3ED. Telephone: 01209 315027. Website: www.nationaltrust.org.uk/east-pool-mine *Interesting old tin mine with a restored steam pumping engine used to keep water out of the deep workings.*

Crofton Pumping Station, Crofton, Marlborough, Wiltshire SN8 3DW. Telephone: 01672 870300. Website: www.croftonbeamengines.org *A rural pumping station built to fill the summit level of the Kennet and Avon Canal and contains the oldest steam engine in the world which still performs its original job.*

Dogdyke Steam Drainage Station, Bridge Farm, Tattershall, Lincolnshire LN4 4JG. Telephone: 01522 683755 (publicity officer). Website: www.dogdyke.com *Original beam engine dating from the 1850s and scoop wheel, which are still run under steam.*

Eastney Beam Engine, Henderson Road, Eastney, Portsmouth, Hampshire PO4 9JF. Telephone: 02392 827261. Website: www.portsmouthmuseums.co.uk/

museum-service/Eastney-Beam-Engine-House *A decorative Victorian building containing a pair of Boulton and Watt beam engines restored to their original condition.*

E17 Pump House Museum, 10 South Access Road, Walthamstow, London E17 8AX. Telephone: 020 8521 1766. Website: www.e17pumphouse.org.uk *An interesting pumping station with a good collection of smaller steam engines and pumps.*

Galton Valley Canal Heritage Centre, Brasshouse Ln, Smethwick, West Midlands, B66 1BA. Telephone: 0121 556 0683. Website: www.sandwell.gov.uk/info/200265/ museums_and_art_gallery/10/our_museums_and_sites/2 *A small museum charting the development of the Birmingham Canals housed in New Smethwick Pumping Station.*

Kempton Steam Museum, Kempton Park Water Treatment Works, Snakey Lane, Hanworth, Middlesex TW13 6XH. Telephone: 01932 765328. Website: www.kemptonsteam.org *The huge triple expansion engine is a must for any fan of steam.*

Levant Mine and Beam Engine, Pendeen, Trewellard, Penzance TR19 7SX. Telephone: 01736 786156. Website: www.nationaltrust.org.uk/ levant-mine-and-beam-engine *The buildings are set upon a dramatic cliff top, and a restored Cornish beam engine is still operated by steam on its original site.*

London Museum of Water and Steam, Green Dragon Lane, Kew Bridge, Brentford, London TW8 0EN. Telephone: 0208 568 4757. Website: www.waterandsteam.org.uk *An excellent collection of working steam engines from pumping stations including the huge 90-foot and 100-foot Cornish engines. Also features artefacts from the water industry and displays showing how the system worked.*

Markfield Beam Engine and Museum, Markfield Road, South Tottenham, London N15 4RB. Telephone: 01707

873628. Website: www.mbeam.org *Beautifully restored compound engine which is supported on eight cast-iron columns so it is independent of the pumping house building.*

Mill Meece Pumping Station, Cotes Heath, Eccleshall, Staffordshire ST21 6QU. Telephone: 01785 822138. Website: www.millmeecepumpingstation.co.uk *A rare example of original horizontal tandem compound steam engines, boilers, and economiser in this Edwardian pumping station.*

Museum of Power, Hatfield Road, Langford, Essex CM9 6QA. Telephone: 01621 843183. Website: www.museumofpower.org.uk *Impressive museum set in an old pumping station with a vast collection of industrial artefacts, a miniature railway and model village; one of its original triple expansion engines is regularly run.*

Papplewick Pumping Station, Rigg Lane, Ravenshead, Nottinghamshire NG15 9AJ. Telephone: 0115 963 2938. Website: www.papplewickpumpingstation.co.uk *One of the finest and most complete Victorian pumping stations with regular demonstrations of its glorious steam engines.*

Pinchbeck Engine Museum, West Marsh Road, Spalding, Lincolnshire PE11 3UW. Telephone: 01775 725861. Website: www.wellandidb.org.uk/museum *This charming little museum houses a 20hp low-pressure steam engine dating from 1833 and other artefacts used in the land drainage of the Fens.*

Prickwillow Museum, Main Street, Prickwillow, Ely, Cambridgeshire CB7 4UN. Telephone: 01353 688360. Website: www.prickwillowmuseum.com *This museum tells the story of the Fenland drainage and houses a number of working diesel engines rescued from pumping stations.*

Ryhope Engines Museum, Waterworks Road, Ryhope, Sunderland SR2 0ND. Telephone: 0191 521 0235. Website: www.ryhopeengines.org.uk *Impressive red brick pumping station complete with working steam engines and boilers.*

Science Museum, London, Exhibition Road, Kensington, London SW7 2DD. Telephone: 0333 241 4000. Website: www.sciencemuseum.org.uk *Includes many original examples of old pumping engines, several of which feature interactive on-screen animated diagrams.*

Stretham Old Engine, Green End, Stretham, Cambridgeshire CB6 3LF. Telephone: 01353 648578. Website: www.strethamoldengine.org.uk *A rare example of an early land drainage steam engine dating from 1831 and its scoop wheel.*

Tees Cottage Museum, Coniscliffe Road, Darlington DL3 8TF. Telephone: 07885 242411 (Hon Secretary). Website: www.teescottage.com *Attractive set of Gothic-style buildings beside the River Tees with its original beam engine and later gas-powered engines on display.*

Twyford Waterworks, Hazeley Road, Twyford, Hampshire SO21 1QA. Telephone: 07516 458900. Website: www.twyfordwaterworks.co.uk *A unique museum featuring a triple expansion steam engine and a water softening plant complete with lime kilns, filter house and a selection of industrial railway locomotives.*

Waterworks Museum, Broomy Hill, Hereford HR4 0LJ. Telephone: 01432 361147. Website: www.waterworksmuseum.org.uk *An interesting museum which not only contains the pumping station but also explores the story of water supply in the area.*

Westonzoyland Pumping Station Museum, Hoopers Lane, Westonzoyland, Somerset TA7 0LS. Telephone: 01278 691595. Website: www.wzlet.org *An excellent example of a drainage pumping station with the largest collection of working stationary steam engines and pumps in the South of England.*

INDEX